The Art of Giving and Receiving Feedback

Shirley Poertner
and
Karen Massetti Miller

PROVANT MEDIA

4601 121ST Street • Urbandale, Iowa 50323
1-888-776-8268 • fax 515-327-2555
www.provantmedia.com

The Art of Giving and Receiving Feedback

Shirley Poertner and Karen Massetti Miller

Copyright ©1996 by American Media Incorporated

This publication is designed to provide accurate and authoritative information in regard to the subject matter covered. It is sold with the understanding that neither the author nor the publisher is engaged in rendering legal, accounting, or other professional service. If legal advice or other expert assistance is required, the services of a competent professional should be sought.

Credits:
American Media Publishing:

Arthur Bauer
Todd McDonald
Esther Vanier

Editor in Chief: Karen Massetti Miller
Designer: Gayle O'Brien
Cover Design: Maura Rombalski

Published by American Media Inc.
4900 University Avenue
West Des Moines, IA 50266-6769

Library of Congress Catalog Card Number 96-84566
Poertner, Shirley and Massetti Miller, Karen
The Art of Giving and Receiving Feedback

Printed in the United States of America
1999
ISBN 1-884926-53-3

Introduction

Good communication tops most people's lists of important workplace skills. Though business offices, retail establishments, and shop floors are relying more and more on complex electronic equipment, not all of the information employees need is found online and in databases. Effective person-to-person communication is more important than ever as teams "form and storm," management becomes more egalitarian, and employees learn to work cross-functionally.

One of the most important person-to-person communication skills is the ability to give and receive feedback effectively. It is also one of the most challenging. No amount of sophisticated technology can diminish the anxiety supervisors, team leaders, and team members can feel when faced with a feedback session. Perhaps you have experienced this sense of apprehension, and that's why you're reading this book.

The good news is that feedback doesn't have to be painful. By learning the proven techniques presented here, you can develop your feedback skills. If you provide feedback to others—coworkers, direct reports, or your manager—this book will help you to present your ideas more effectively. It will also help you to be a better receiver of feedback, even feedback that is presented awkwardly. With just a little practice, you'll be able to turn feedback sessions into tools that can help you and your coworkers improve your job performance and meet important goals. Good luck!

About the Authors

Shirley Poertner

Shirley Poertner is the president of Poertner Consulting Group, a consulting and training firm specializing in organizational development and individual learning. She has more than 15 years of experience in the training and development field.

Before starting her own company in 1995, Ms. Poertner held key management positions with Pioneer Hi-Bred International, Inc., Meredith Corporation, and First Interstate of Iowa, Inc. (now Boatmen's Bancshares of Iowa, Inc.). She has worked with numerous Fortune 500 companies, as well as with smaller organizations, public-sector agencies, and not-for-profits to assess and meet their development needs.

Having spent several years of her career as Vice President of Human Resources, Ms. Poertner understands the importance of giving and receiving clear and specific feedback in the workplace. She has coached supervisors and team leaders in delivering important information to their employees and team members. She has conducted workshops to help employees and team members give and receive feedback effectively with their colleagues and leaders. Ms. Poertner knows the intricacies of effective feedback and conveys them as a dedicated coach.

Karen Massetti Miller is the editor in chief of American Media's How-To Book Series. Ms. Miller has taught college-level courses in public speaking, business and professional communication, and journalism and has created a variety of training programs for print and electronic media. Her experience as both a teacher and a practitioner of business and professional communication has given her insight into the nature and importance of effective feedback.

Acknowledgments

The authors wish to thank Todd McDonald and Esther Vanier at American Media for their help, support, and assistance with this book.

Assessing Your Current Feedback Skills

How to Get the Most from This Book

This book is designed to help you improve your skills in giving and receiving feedback in the workplace. To get the most from this book, as you read, think about the ways in which you give and receive feedback. Ask yourself if you recognize your own behaviors in our examples and if there are feedback skills you can develop further. To help you identify skills you would like to improve, here are two self-assessments to evaluate your current feedback skills—one for how you give feedback and another for how you receive it.

How Well Do I Give Feedback?

This self-assessment will help you measure your current skills in giving feedback. For each statement, check "rarely," "sometimes," or "often" to indicate how consistently you use the described behavior in the workplace.

	Rarely	Sometimes	Often
1. I pick an appropriate time and place to give feedback.	_____	_____	_____
2. I keep my emotions in check, remaining calm and keeping my voice even.	_____	_____	_____
3. I provide specific, detailed information about the employee's behavior or performance.	_____	_____	_____
4. I explain the impact the employee's actions are having on the team or organization.	_____	_____	_____
5. I really listen to the responses of those receiving my feedback.	_____	_____	_____
6. I clarify my expectations if there is any confusion about the behavior in question.	_____	_____	_____
7. I remember to thank and encourage the receivers of my feedback.	_____	_____	_____
8. I provide input as needed in developing an action plan for meeting behavioral or performance goals.	_____	_____	_____
9. I focus on the steps of the feedback process to keep the dialogue on track.	_____	_____	_____
10. I try to understand feedback from the other person's point of view and preferred communication style.	_____	_____	_____

Of course, giving feedback is only half of the story. Take a moment now and assess your skills as a feedback recipient.

How Well Do I Receive Feedback?

This self-assessment will help you measure your current skills in receiving feedback. For each statement, check "rarely," "sometimes," or "often" to indicate how consistently you use the described behavior in the workplace.

	Rarely	Sometimes	Often
1. I truly listen to what feedback givers are saying.	_____	_____	_____
2. I keep feedback in perspective and don't overreact.	_____	_____	_____
3. I try to learn from all feedback, even if it's poorly given.	_____	_____	_____
4. I am willing to admit to and learn from questions about my performance or behavior at work.	_____	_____	_____
5. Rather than avoiding feedback, I attempt to turn every feedback session into a useful encounter.	_____	_____	_____
6. I accept redirection and reinforcement rather than denying them.	_____	_____	_____
7 I accept responsibility for my role in achieving individual, team, and organizational goals.	_____	_____	_____
8. I accept responsibility for searching for solutions to performance and behavioral problems that threaten goals.	_____	_____	_____
9. I accept responsibility for keeping my emotions in check during feedback discussions.	_____	_____	_____
10. I am committed to listening and learning in all feedback situations.	_____	_____	_____

How Did You Score?

How did you score on the two self-assessments? If you answered most of the questions with "often," your skills for giving useful feedback and receiving feedback effectively are well developed.

If you answered a number of questions with "rarely" or "sometimes," your feedback skills could probably use further development.

At the end of this book, we will provide an opportunity for you to reassess your skills and develop an action plan for strengthening those areas in which you need more experience.

Table of Contents

Chapter *One*

The Power of Feedback

Chapter Objectives

▶ Define feedback.

▶ Recognize ineffective types of feedback.

▶ Recognize the characteristics of effective feedback.

▶ Define redirection and reinforcement, two types of feedback that are especially effective in the workplace.

What Is Feedback?

A division manager hands in a report to her area director and waits for a month without receiving a reaction. The division manager wonders, "What did I do wrong?"

■ A supervisor becomes upset at a secretary who consistently makes typing errors. "Don't you know anything about the English language?" he yells. "It's amazing you ever finished high school!" The manager slams a recently typed memo on the secretary's desk and stalks off; the specific typing errors are never discussed.

■ An employee receives praise from a supervisor during an annual evaluation. "You're doing a great job," she's told. "Keep up the good work." As the employee leaves the supervisor's office, she wonders, "What exactly am I doing well? I want to keep doing it, but I'm not sure what 'it' is."

Whenever we respond to another person, we are giving that person feedback. We may be reacting to any number of things:

◆ The way a person looks

◆ His or her actions

Whenever we respond to another person, we are giving that person feedback.

- Something he or she said

- Or a combination of factors

Similarly, our feedback may take many forms. We may state our reactions verbally, through speaking or writing, or we may react nonverbally, letting our body language and facial expressions speak for us.

Though there are many types of feedback, not all feedback is useful. Consider our three examples. In the first example, the area director has responded to the division manager with silence. Silence is actually one of the most common forms of feedback in business. How many times have you heard a manager say, "You won't hear from me unless there's a problem"? But silence can be misinterpreted. In this case, the division manager has interpreted silence as criticism, but is that what the area director really means? The area director may just have thought she was too busy to respond, yet her silence has sent a message that is unintentionally negative.

Silence certainly wasn't a problem for the manager in the second example. That manager chose to give feedback in the form of criticism, attacking the secretary's personal qualities rather than focusing on the typing errors. The manager may have vented some emotion by yelling at the secretary, but the secretary still has no idea what the errors are and what should be done about them. The manager's criticism has only created distrust and hostility, which will make it even more difficult to discuss the actual problem.

> **Though there are many types of feedback, not all feedback is useful.**

The supervisor in our third example offered praise, certainly a more pleasant form of feedback than the first two. The employee in the third example is undoubtedly happy to learn that her boss likes her work, but unless she asks for more specific details regarding what actions she should continue, the praise is of little long-term value.

As you can see, we are constantly responding to the actions of others, sometimes even without meaning to—as the old cliché says, "You cannot not communicate." How can we ensure that our responses provide people with useful feedback? Our first step is to determine what we want our feedback to accomplish.

Take a Moment

Did our opening examples remind you of a similar situation you may have encountered? Describe the situation.

_____

_____

_____

_____

Do you think the situation you experienced was handled well? How might it have been handled better?

_____

_____

_____

_____

How Do We Give Feedback in the Workplace?

In the workplace, our feedback takes on special meaning. In this book, we will define *workplace feedback* as information we provide fellow employees and team members about their acts in order to help them meet individual, group, and organizational goals. In the workplace, there are two types of acts about which we generally provide feedback: job performance and work-related behavior.

1

- *Job performance* involves competency—whether or not an employee is capably performing specific tasks that have been assigned.

- *Work-related behavior* involves the way in which an employee performs his or her tasks—whether he or she speaks politely to customers, for example, and works cooperatively with other team members.

> *Workplace feedback* is information we provide fellow employees about their job performance and their work-related behavior in order to help them meet goals.

Notice that our definition of workplace feedback is fairly specific. When we give workplace feedback, we are not commenting on our coworkers' personalities or private lives, nor are we dwelling on employees' past errors in order to punish them. Instead, we respond to those factors that affect our feedback recipient's work or the work of others so that our recipient can plan for the future.

What is the best way to give workplace feedback? As we have seen, not all types of information result in effective feedback. The feedback given in our first three examples produced a variety of results. Silence allowed the division manager to create her own interpretation of the area supervisor's reaction, which may or may not have been correct. Criticism created harsh feelings between the secretary and the manager. Praise created positive feelings during the employee evaluation but accomplished nothing more. What could more effective feedback have done?

Redirection and Reinforcement

Think for a moment about our last two examples. Did the manager really want to insult the secretary? No, the criticism was meant to *redirect* the secretary's job performance to eliminate the typing errors—it just came out badly. And what was the intention of the supervisor in the second example? To *reinforce* the employee's positive actions so that she will repeat and develop them.

These two types of feedback—redirection and reinforcement—are especially effective in the workplace.

◆ **Redirection**—identifies job-related behaviors and performance that do not contribute to individual, group, and organizational goals and helps the employee develop alternative strategies.

◆ **Reinforcement**—identifies job-related behaviors and performance that contribute to individual, group, and organizational goals and encourages the employee to repeat and develop them.

Redirection and reinforcement are really two halves of the same coin.

Redirection and reinforcement are really two halves of the same coin—they work together to provide all members of an organization with the information they need to improve their job performance and work up to their full potential. When feedback takes the form of redirection and reinforcement, it has a number of useful characteristics:

◆ It is focused on acts, not attitude.

◆ It is directed toward the future.

◆ It is goal oriented.

◆ It is multidirectional.

◆ It is supportive.

◆ It is continual.

Useful Feedback Is Focused on Acts, Not Attitude

Useful workplace feedback focuses on acts rather than an employee's attitude or personal characteristics—it responds to specific actions that are done in the process of performing one's job. Attacking someone's talent and abilities, educational background, physical attributes, or ethnic background is not useful feedback and, in extreme cases, could leave your organization subject to legal action.

Sometimes we may think that we are giving a person feedback about his or her actions when, in fact, we are commenting on attitude, which is not a useful type of feedback. It does little good to accuse an employee of being "unenthusiastic" or "unprofessional"—we have no way of knowing how that person truly feels, nor is it really our business. Instead, we should focus on what we can see—the acts that we hope to redirect or reinforce. Rather than commenting on an employee's lack of professionalism, for example, we redirect job performance issues, like typing errors, and behavioral problems that affect job performance, like lateness.

> **1**
>
> Useful feedback responds to specific actions that are done in the process of performing one's job.

Take a Moment

Think of a situation in which you received redirection that was not focused on acts (as in the secretarial example at the beginning of this chapter). Describe the criticism you received. How did the other person approach you? What did he or she say?

_____

_____

How did you respond to this criticism? Were there aspects of your work that could have been improved? How could your critic have changed his or her message so that you could have benefited from the advice by redirecting your efforts?

_____

_____

Useful Feedback Is Directed Toward the Future

The purpose of feedback is not to dwell on the past—it is to plan for the future. Though feedback begins with a consideration of past and current behaviors and job performance, it certainly doesn't end there. Useful feedback uses past actions as a springboard to help the feedback recipient develop effective plans for future actions.

Useful Feedback Is Goal Oriented

Everyone within your organization shares common goals that relate to your organization's mission, vision, and strategies for success. Members of your team or department share certain goals as well. Similarly, everyone in your organization has individual goals that will help him or her contribute to the company's goals.

We might think of individual goals as paths all leading to the completion of organizational goals. As each of us walks along our path, we believe that we are moving in the right direction. But there may be obstacles ahead that we can't see, or perhaps our path is interfering with someone else's. The only way we will ever know these things is if people from other vantage points tell us. When we look at feedback this way, it becomes as important a work tool as a computer or a calculator.

Take a Moment

Think of an instance when a colleague or a supervisor provided feedback from his or her vantage point that helped get you back on track toward meeting an important goal. Describe the instance. What was the goal and how did the feedback help you?

_____

_____

_____

_____

1

Useful Feedback Is Multidirectional

Many of us might think of feedback as hierarchical in nature: a manager or supervisor sends feedback downward to an employee, not the other way around. But feedback is multidirectional. In a hierarchical organization, employees need to send feedback upward to managers; otherwise, management will have no way of knowing what is actually happening on the front lines. Employees also need to provide feedback laterally to coworkers so that problems can be corrected immediately instead of waiting for management to respond.

As cross-functional teams have become more common, ongoing feedback among all team members is especially important. Because every member of the team has a different perspective, each person has a unique vantage point and insight into the work situation. Sharing information from one perspective can help other team members see things they might not have seen from their vantage points. It is everyone's responsibility to share his or her unique insights in order to help the team meet its goal.

> **It is everyone's responsibility to share his or her unique insights in order to help the team meet its goal.**

Take a Moment

Whose behavior or performance affects how you are able to do your job? Certainly your manager. Who else? List them below by position or role. (Don't forget to include those external to your workplace, as well as internal contacts.)

_____   _____

_____   _____

_____   _____

1. Identify with a * the role you would be most likely to provide with reinforcing feedback.

2. Identify with a # the role you would be most likely to provide with redirecting feedback.

Useful Feedback Is Supportive

Useful feedback is given in a spirit of supportiveness. The sole purpose of giving workplace feedback is to help associates, supervisors, and coworkers to improve the quality of their work in order to meet goals—it is always given with helpfulness in mind. Feedback should never be given in a way that belittles the recipient or makes others look good at that person's expense.

Useful Feedback Is Continual

Feedback isn't just something we provide during an annual review or some other type of formal evaluation. In order to do our jobs in the best way possible, we need continual information about our job-related behaviors and performance. We need to know immediately when we should redirect our efforts so that simple mistakes don't become costly errors, and we need reinforcement when those changes have been successful so that we continue to develop a specific action.

When feedback is continual, team members feel comfortable responding to each other on an ongoing basis.

When feedback is continual, team members feel comfortable responding to each other on an ongoing basis. As we develop solutions to specific situations, redirecting feedback will become reinforcing feedback, and each new piece of information will bring us closer to meeting our individual and group goals, as in Diagram 1.

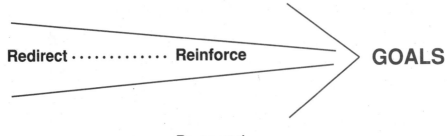

Redirect · · · · · · · · · · · Reinforce   GOALS

DIAGRAM 1

Misperceptions About Feedback

As useful as feedback can be, many of us are reluctant to give or receive it. Usually that reluctance is based on misperceptions we have about feedback. Though we are learning to see feedback in a more positive light, many people still associate feedback with hurtful criticism. They are reluctant to hurt the feelings of others, and they certainly don't want their own work to be criticized. Perhaps you can recall times in your life when you have been the subject of hurtful criticism, or times when your criticism, no matter how well intentioned, seemed to hurt the feelings of another.

Many people still associate feedback with hurtful criticism.

When we think about instances in which we have been subjected to hurtful criticism, we often find that what hurt us wasn't the fact that someone was commenting on our work, but the way in which those comments were offered. Somehow, feedback about our typing errors turned into an evaluation of our entire educational history and personality.

As we've seen, effective feedback doesn't veer off into these types of unstructured statements. By following the steps in this guide, you will be able to provide feedback that avoids hurtful criticism, and you will be able to respond to any hurtful criticism you may receive so that it, too, becomes useful.

Sharing the Benefits of Continual Feedback

When everyone on your team learns to provide and expect feedback that is focused on acts, directed toward the future, goal oriented, multidirectional, supportive, and continual, you will find that feedback sessions become opportunities for creative problem solving rather than dreaded encounters. Everyone on your team will share the same language, and you will be able to share ideas without fear of hurt feelings or reprisals.

Even as you are beginning to realize that continual feedback can have a number of benefits for you and your organization, you still may not be totally comfortable with the idea. In our next chapter, we will explore some of the common misperceptions that keep people from giving feedback.

Self-ChecK: Chapter 1 Review

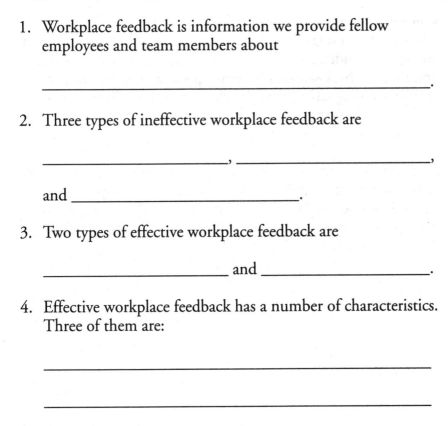

Suggested answers appear on page 100.

Suggested answers appear on page 100.

1. Workplace feedback is information we provide fellow employees and team members about

   _____.

2. Three types of ineffective workplace feedback are

   _____, _____,

   and _____.

3. Two types of effective workplace feedback are

   _____ and _____.

4. Effective workplace feedback has a number of characteristics. Three of them are:

   _____

   _____

   _____

Chapter *Two*

Useful Feedback Is Detailed Feedback

Chapter Objectives

▶ Understand the importance of detailed feedback.

▶ Recognize the features of detailed feedback.

▶ Recognize the roles that those giving and receiving feedback play in creating detailed feedback.

Creating Detailed Feedback

In Chapter 1 we defined workplace feedback as information we provide fellow employees and team members about their job performance and their work-related behavior in order to help them meet individual, group, and organizational goals. We've already seen that the nature of that information helps determine whether our feedback will be effective or not: useful feedback focuses on acts rather than attitudes, is goal oriented, and is always given in a spirit of mutual support.

Feedback is most helpful when it provides as much detailed information about our actions as possible.

A key feature that helps make feedback useful is the amount of detail it provides. Feedback is most helpful when it provides as much detailed information about our actions as possible. We can make sure that feedback is detailed by remembering these simple guidelines:

◆ Detailed feedback is *specific*.

◆ Detailed feedback is *accurate*.

◆ Detailed feedback is *inquiring*.

Detailed Feedback Is Specific

■ "I just don't like the way you arranged that display. Change it!"

■ "The ad copy you wrote just doesn't 'click.'
You know what I mean."

■ "Try to put a little more 'oomph' in your presentations.
Wake people up!"

2

You've probably heard statements like these before. They are attempts at redirection, but they're poor ones. They don't give the person receiving the feedback enough specific information to make changes in his or her actions. The most the receiver can do in each case is to try again, but without specific information, that attempt will be just another shot in the dark. The receiver may have to make several attempts before he or she hits on something the person giving the feedback likes. This is a waste of time and resources as well as a drain on morale.

You can avoid situations like this by making your feedback as specific as possible. Before giving feedback to another person, try to recall as much specific information as you can about the action you want to redirect or reinforce. You might begin by asking yourself what, when, where, who, and how:

◆ *What* happened?

◆ *Where* and *when* did it occur?

◆ *Who* was involved?

◆ *How* did it affect others?

> **Before giving feedback to another person, try to recall as much specific information as you can about the action you want to redirect or reinforce.**

With these questions in mind, consider this alternative to our third example:

■ "Your presentations always include a wealth of new ideas, but you don't sound personally excited about the things you're suggesting. Your voice is often very soft and monotone, and your rate of speaking can be very slow. Our surveys show that your audience members think you sound bored with your topic, and that makes them feel bored, too. Are there some things you could do to make your enthusiasm for your topic more evident to your listeners?"

This revised example tells the feedback recipient specifically what he's been doing (not projecting enthusiasm for his material), where and when he's been doing it (during presentations), who it involves (his listeners), and how it affects them (makes them feel bored). The recipient will be able to redirect his efforts with much less confusion and effort than if he had received the feedback in our earlier example.

It is also important to be specific when giving reinforcing feedback as well. Consider the difference between these two statements:

■ "Great report, Kari. Keep up the good work."

■ "I liked the way you incorporated the two graphs into your report this month, Kari. They made it much easier to follow the cash flow. I hope you'll do it again."

Kari will be better able to repeat her report-writing efforts based on the specific information in the second example.

Detailed Feedback Is Accurate

Feedback can do little good if it inaccurately portrays the action in question. Describing actions that were never taken or events that never occurred only puts your feedback recipient on the defensive as he or she attempts to describe what really took place.

Always be sure that you have an accurate understanding of the situation you are describing before you begin a feedback session. If you think that there might be some question about your version of the situation, try to identify more than one instance of it and document times, dates, and locations. You can also check your observations against those of others to see if you all arrive at similar interpretations.

Detailed Feedback Is Inquiring

Have an inquiring mind—learn all that you can about a complicated situation before you give feedback. Your investigation may help you arrive at a totally different interpretation of the situation—an interpretation that could result in totally different feedback. You may even discover that you wish to direct your feedback to a different person, or that actions that you thought needed to be changed were actually making a positive contribution.

Continue to ask questions during the feedback process itself. Encourage your feedback recipient to describe events that may be affecting the situation in question, and involve him or her in developing any plans for future action.

2

Always be sure that you have an accurate understanding of the situation before you begin a feedback session.

Take a Moment

Effective feedback is specific. How could the person giving the following feedback have been more specific in reinforcing or redirecting the other person's performance or behavior?

"Pat, this report is not clear."

_____

_____

"Lee, your presentation seemed to drag."

_____

_____

"Dee, your team seems to be jelling nicely."

_____

_____

Effective feedback is inquiring. Describe an instance when your inquiries—either prior to or during a feedback discussion—resulted in information which greatly changed the focus of the feedback you planned to deliver.

_____

_____

_____

_____

Don't Let Time Dull Your Details

Time has a way of dulling even the most vivid memories. In order to incorporate as many details into your feedback as possible, try to give redirection or reinforcement as close as possible to the time the act in question actually occurred. It is always easier to discuss something when events are fresh in everyone's mind, and responding to a situation quickly shows that you believe that it is important.

One exception to this rule is the situation in which you need to both reinforce and redirect the person receiving the feedback. People receiving both types of feedback generally focus on the redirection, and the reinforcement that you wanted to provide often is ignored.

To alleviate this confusion, try splitting your feedback. One effective method of splitting feedback involves giving reinforcement as soon after the action in question as possible, then providing redirection closer to the time the person is going to repeat the action. For example, a manager who has just received a monthly report could reinforce her associate's use of charts and bar graphs immediately after receiving the report and then redirect the associate to also include a spreadsheet with the report closer to next month's due date.

A word of caution—balance the need for a timely response against the need to prepare for the feedback session. Remember that your feedback needs to be well organized and documented as well as on time. Beginning to plan your feedback as soon as you realize that a situation requires your response will help you to be both on time and well prepared.

2

Give redirection or reinforcement as close as possible to the time the act in question actually occurred.

Specifiying is providing more and more specific information to the person receiving your feedback.

Feedback—A Two-Way Process

Giving Feedback: The Process of Specifying

Keeping these guidelines in mind as you prepare your feedback will help you develop redirection and reinforcement that is detailed and useful. As you begin your first feedback sessions, you might think of giving detailed feedback as the process of *specifying*—that is, providing more and more specific information to the person receiving your feedback. The more specific the information you can provide, the closer your recipient can come to meeting individual, group, and organizational goals.

Of course, creating useful feedback isn't only the responsibility of the person giving that feedback. Both those giving feedback and those receiving it have important roles to play in ensuring that feedback provides as much useful detail as possible.

Receiving Feedback: The Process of Probing

Probing is asking the person giving you feedback for more and more details.

It's a fact of life—you won't always receive useful, detailed feedback on the job. But that doesn't mean you have to accept poor quality feedback that does nothing to help you redirect or reinforce your own performance. Feedback recipients can request the details they need through the process of *probing*— asking the person giving the feedback for more and more details. As you probe for information, you will receive more and more specific details about your behavior and performance.

Diagram 2 illustrates how the processes of specifying and probing work together to bring ever-increasing amounts of information to the feedback situation. As the levels of probing and specifying increase, so does the level of detailed information available to the person receiving the feedback, which will help that person move closer to achieving goals.

ACHIEVING GOALS

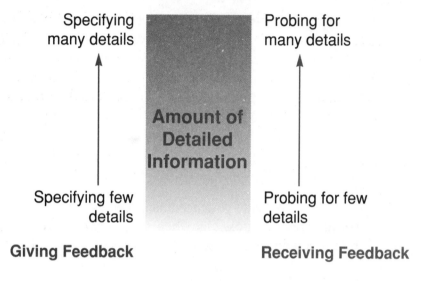

DIAGRAM 2

In the following chapters, we will outline specific techniques that will help you to be an efficient giver and receiver of feedback. In each case, we will stress the importance of specifying—and probing for—the amount of specific information necessary to redirect or reinforce behaviors and performance.

Self-Check: Chapter 2 Review

Suggested answers appear on page 100.

1. What are three characteristics of detailed feedback?

   _____

   _____

   _____

2. In order to provide your feedback recipient with as much specific detail as possible, when should you provide reinforcement or redirection?

   _____

   _____

3. Providing more and more specific information to the recipient of your feedback is the process of

   _____

4. Asking the person giving you feedback for more and more details is the process of

   _____

Chapter *Three*

Planning Effective Feedback

Chapter Objectives

▶ Recognize the importance of planning feedback.

▶ Ask yourself a series of questions that will help you prepare detailed feedback.

Why You Should Plan Your Feedback

Effective feedback doesn't just happen. Whether you're giving redirection or reinforcement, you should plan what you are going to say in advance. You will need to identify examples to support the redirection or reinforcement you want to give, and you will need to organize your thoughts so that you are able to present your feedback coherently.

As you take part in more and more feedback sessions, you may find that, in some cases, you actually spend more time planning your feedback than you do giving it. This is not uncommon— the more time you put into your planning, the more smoothly your feedback sessions will run.

Ask These Questions When Planning Feedback

Knowing that you want to give someone reinforcement or redirection is just the beginning of the feedback planning process. Try asking yourself this series of questions to get your feedback planning on track.

◆ Can I identify and accurately describe the behavior or performance I want to redirect or reinforce and its effects on others in the organization?

◆ Do I have detailed examples of the act and its effects that I can use to support my descriptions?

◆ Can I identify and describe the results that I hope my reinforcement or redirection will produce?

◆ Does the person receiving the feedback understand my expectations for his or her performance?

◆ Is the person receiving the feedback really responsible for the act in question?

◆ Is the other person open to receiving feedback from me?

◆ Have I put off giving this feedback for a long time?

◆ Have I given myself enough time to prepare the feedback?

3

Begin your feedback preparation by identifying the specific job performance or behavior issue you want to redirect or reinforce and the effects that act has on others in your organization.

Identifying Behavior and Performance Issues

Can you identify and accurately describe the specific behavior or performance you want to redirect or reinforce and its effects on others in the organization? As we saw in Chapter 2, effective feedback requires more than just a vague statement that you like or dislike someone's work. Statements like "Something's wrong here—I don't know exactly what it is, but change it" don't provide enough details for employees to begin to redirect their actions. Likewise, telling someone, "Keep up the good work!" does little to tell that person what good work is.

Begin your feedback preparation by identifying the specific job performance or behavior issue you want to redirect or reinforce and the effects that act has on others in your organization. Prepare for your feedback sessions by making a list in which you describe the act and its effects, as in these two examples:

Kelsey:

Behavior to Redirect:	Was late to work 3 times in the past week.
Effects on Others:	Person on previous shift had to work late; people on same shift are irritated and demoralized.

Word-Processing Pool:

Performance to Reinforce:	Reorganized work process so that correspondence is completed more quickly and with fewer errors.
Effects on Others:	Lower turnaround time means we can respond to clients more quickly; reduction in errors means fewer documents have to be retyped, which also saves time and money.

Providing Examples

Do you have detailed examples of the act and its effects that you can use to support your argument? The more examples you can describe, the stronger your case will be, especially if you are asking someone to redirect an action and are concerned that the person might resist your redirection. Here is one way you could list examples of actions and effects to support redirection of the employee who is late to work:

Kelsey:

Example of Behavior:	Effects on Others:
Monday: Kelsey 1/2 hour late for first shift.	Pam had to open by herself.
Wednesday: Kelsey 20 minutes late getting back from lunch.	Pam had to delay lunch break; front desk short-staffed at busiest time of day.
Thursday: Kelsey 1 hour late for second shift.	John had to continue working after first shift ended.

3

Identifying Desired Results

Remember, the purpose of giving feedback isn't to dwell on the past—it's to plan for the future. Can you identify and describe the results that you hope your reinforcement or redirection will produce? After you give your feedback, what types of actions do you hope to see?

> After you give your feedback, what types of actions do you hope to see?

In the case of reinforcement, the answer is easy—you hope to see the act in question repeated and developed. In the case of redirection, you may need to give a little more thought to this question. Although you will want to take input from the person receiving your redirection about specific short- and long-term goals, you should have some objectives in mind. Keep these goals in sight as you talk to the person to ensure that the action plan you negotiate leads to the results you want.

Understanding Expectations

Does the person receiving the feedback understand your expectations for his or her behavior and job performance? This is an especially important question for cases of redirection. Often we assume that people understand exactly what they are supposed to be doing in a given situation, but that may not be the case. Ask yourself what you and others have done in the past to clarify your expectations. Refer to the person's job description and to previous performance evaluations—have your expectations ever been addressed before?

If you discover that no one has ever addressed the act in question with your feedback recipient, your redirection may take the form of clarifying your expectations. If the expectations are new to the employee, you may also need to discuss such questions as:

- ◆ Are the expectations fair and reasonable?

- ◆ Is the feedback recipient capable of meeting them?

- ◆ Are there ways in which the team can help the feedback recipient meet the expectations?

Controlling the Situation

Is the person receiving the feedback really responsible for the act in question? The person to whom you are planning to give your feedback may have no trouble understanding your expectations yet be unable to meet them. This could occur for a variety of reasons. Perhaps the feedback recipient is not actually responsible for the situation you are addressing, or perhaps the recipient does not have the resources to redirect or repeat his or her actions.

> **Ask yourself what you and others have done in the past to clarify expectations.**

Before you give feedback to anyone, try to discover if other people might be responsible for the situation. You may want to reinforce Ben's addition of bar graphs to the weekly sales memo, but he can only do this when accounting gives him the figures. Perhaps Anita in accounting needs your reinforcement, too.

If you think outside factors may be affecting your feedback recipient's actions, but you aren't sure, ask the recipient in the course of giving your feedback and take his or her response into account as the two of you develop plans for the future.

Accepting Feedback

3

Is the other person open to accepting feedback from you? This will depend on your relationship with the person receiving your feedback and his or her attitude toward the feedback process. Questions to ask yourself include:

◆ **Are you a credible feedback source for this person?**
Does your feedback recipient believe that you have the expertise to provide competent redirection or reinforcement? If you believe your credibility may be an issue, make doubly sure you have plenty of examples to support your comments.

◆ **Is your relationship with your feedback recipient cordial?**
People are always willing to accept suggestions more readily from someone with whom they have a good working relationship. If you do not have a good relationship with your receiver, or perhaps have criticized (rather than redirected) the receiver's work in the past, you may need to reestablish your relationship before feedback can be effective.

> People are always willing to accept suggestions more readily from someone with whom they have a good working relationship.

◆ **What is your status relative to the feedback recipient's?**
In hierarchical organizations, it is often difficult to give feedback, especially redirection, to a manager or supervisor. If you are presenting feedback to a higher-up, present plenty of examples to establish your credibility and remember to present your comments as supportive rather than critical.

Delaying Feedback

Have you put off giving this feedback for a long time? If you previously looked on feedback as unpleasant or unimportant, you may have put off approaching the receiver with your feedback. Unfortunately, delaying feedback makes it harder to give that feedback when you finally do sit down with your receiver.

◆ If you have delayed giving redirection, the situation may have had time to escalate from a minor glitch to a serious problem.

◆ If you have delayed giving reinforcement, your recipient may not remember the act in question and may wonder why it has taken you so long to respond.

◆ The receiver of your feedback may not be open to your input after such a long delay. Delayed redirection can often result in responses like "But that's the way we've always done it" from the recipient.

You may need to explain to your feedback recipient that you realize that you have not always been timely in giving feedback, and that this is your first effort to correct that problem. Don't delay—if you have been avoiding a feedback session, don't put it off any longer! Immediately schedule a session and start to prepare for it.

Taking Time for Feedback

Have you given yourself enough time to prepare your feedback? Don't kid yourself—it takes time to think about all of the issues we've just mentioned as well as to document and describe the actions you hope to redirect or reinforce. Always give yourself enough time so that you begin every feedback session fully prepared.

Always give yourself enough time so that you begin every feedback session fully prepared.

3

Take a Moment

Think of someone in your workplace to whom you need to give feedback about the quality of his or her efforts. Perhaps you need to redirect that person's performance. Perhaps there's a behavior that is inappropriate or unsatisfactory.

Use the Feedback Plan form on the following page to help you prepare the necessary feedback. If you take the time to consider each of the questions, you should be fully prepared for your next feedback session.

Our next chapter will describe a series of steps that will guide you through the feedback process.

Feedback Plan

Identify and accurately describe the specific actions you want to reinforce or redirect and their effects on others.

_____

_____

List detailed examples of these actions and their effects to use as support for question #1.

_____

_____

Identify and describe the results that you hope your reinforcement or redirection will produce.

_____

_____

Do you think the person receiving the feedback understands your expectations for his/her behavior or performance?

_____ Yes _____ No

Do you think the person receiving the feedback is really responsible for the behavior or performance in question?

_____ Yes _____ No

Do you think the other person is open to receiving feedback from you?

_____ Yes _____ No

Have you put off giving this feedback for a long time?

_____ Yes _____ No

Have you given yourself enough time to prepare the feedback?

_____ Yes _____ No

Self-Check: Chapter 3 Review

Suggested answers appear on page 100.

1. True or False?
   You may find yourself putting more time into planning your feedback than you do actually giving it.

2. True or False?
   It isn't necessary to identify and describe specific actions that you want to redirect or reinforce—just stating that you like or dislike someone's work is enough.

3. True or False?
   You should always be sure that your feedback recipient understands your expectations for his or her performance before you begin a feedback session.

4. True or False?
   Before you begin a feedback session, you should be sure that the person you will be redirecting or reinforcing is actually responsible for the action in question.

5. True or False?
   Delayed feedback is no more difficult to give than timely feedback.

3

Chapter *Four*

Steps for Giving Effective Feedback

Chapter Objectives

▶ Follow the basic steps for reinforcing effective job performance and job-related behavior.

▶ Follow the basic steps for redirecting ineffective job performance and job-related behavior.

▶ Understand how the amount of information you give your feedback recipient can help that person achieve individual, group, and organizational goals.

Preparing to Give Your Feedback

If you've done everything you can to plan your feedback, giving that feedback should be relatively easy. You can begin the process by choosing the time and place to present your feedback.

Choosing an Appropriate Time and Place

Try to give your feedback in a situation where you won't be distracted by other people or concerns. Plan ahead and make an appointment with your feedback recipient—try to choose a time when neither of you will be too tired or stressed.

If you are giving redirection, you will want to choose a private place where your conversation won't be overheard. If you are giving the same redirection to a group of people, such as instructing a group of telemarketers on a better way to ask callers to hold, you can present your comments to the entire group. However, under most circumstances, you should not redirect an individual in front of other employees.

Reinforcement can sometimes be given more informally. If your comments will be brief, you might ask the person to step inside your office for a moment rather than scheduling a formal appointment. If your organizational culture supports public recognition of employees, you can give reinforcement in front of others, such as during a weekly staff meeting. This can be an effective way of recognizing an accomplishment as well as demonstrating to other employees the type of actions you want to reinforce.

> **Under most circumstances, you should not redirect an individual in front of other employees.**

4

Beginning the Feedback Session

Whether you are redirecting or reinforcing an associate or coworker, try to help that person feel comfortable as you begin the feedback session. If the feedback session is taking place in your office, invite the other person to sit down. Offer him or her coffee or a soft drink if that is customary within your organization. If the other person seems especially nervous, you might try to break the ice with some casual conversation before getting into your topic.

As your feedback session progresses, keep your own emotions in check, especially if you are attempting to redirect a problem that has frustrated you in the past. Your demeanor sets the tone for the meeting—do not say or do anything that would cause the person receiving your feedback to become emotional. Remain calm and keep your voice even throughout the session—never shout at or berate an employee.

Presenting Your Feedback

Once you have established a positive tone for the feedback session, the process should flow smoothly. Remember that your goal is to specify as much detailed, useful information as possible to help your associate or coworker be as productive as possible. You can do that easily by following some basic steps for reinforcement and redirection.

Basic Steps for Giving Reinforcement

You can give reinforcement that your associates and coworkers will remember if you follow these four easy steps:

1. Describe the behavior or performance you want to reinforce.

2. Explain the positive impact that act has had on the organization.

3. Help your feedback recipient take credit for his or her success.

4. Thank your feedback recipient for his or her contribution toward meeting group or organizational goals and encourage similar future actions.

The steps for giving reinforcement are summarized in the following flowchart.

Steps for Giving Reinforcement

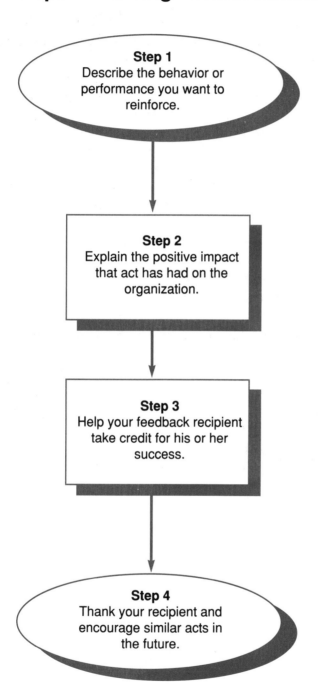

Step 1
Describe the behavior or performance you want to reinforce.

Step 2
Explain the positive impact that act has had on the organization.

4

Step 3
Help your feedback recipient take credit for his or her success.

Step 4
Thank your recipient and encourage similar acts in the future.

Step 1—Describe the Behavior or Performance You Want to Reinforce

The more detail you are able to give employees in the course of reinforcement, the better they will be able to repeat and build on their work.

You should begin any reinforcement session with a description of the behavior or performance you would like to reinforce. Remember, the purpose of giving reinforcement isn't just to make the other person feel good, it's to describe the act you want to reinforce in such a way that the person receiving the feedback will be able to repeat it. The more detail you are able to give employees in the course of reinforcement, the better they will be able to repeat and build on their work. Consider these two sets of examples: Which responses do you think give the receivers of the feedback enough information to repeat their performance?

1. "Thanks for reorganizing the files, Cindy. They look great!"

   "I'm very impressed with the way you've reorganized the files, Cindy. Organizing the files by dates makes them much easier to find, and I especially like the way you put the frequently used files on the bottom where we can all reach them."

2. "Thanks for working overtime last night to proofread the report, June. I hope it didn't keep you up too late."

   "Thanks for the extra effort you put into proofreading the report this month, June. I especially appreciate the time you took to check all of the profit and loss figures—I notice you caught several significant errors."

In each example, the receivers of the second response will know exactly what they should do they next time they perform these tasks.

Step 2—Explain the Behavior's Positive Impact

Most of us like to know how our efforts fit into the big picture. Learning how our work supports the work of others helps us to see our importance to the group.

Explaining the positive impact an employee's actions have had on the team or organization can help that person see the value of his or her contribution and create extra incentive to repeat and develop that act. Again, the more information you can give the employee about the effect of his or her contribution, the more valuable your feedback will be. Consider the following example:

> **Learning how our work supports the work of others helps us to see our importance to the group.**

- "I know that with so many employees out sick this month, it took extra effort for you to get the quarterly report out on time. Thanks to your efforts, management had the information they needed to make some important decisions about hiring and compensation; in fact, they approved the new assistant we've been hoping for in this division."

4

The employee receiving this reinforcement will know exactly how her hard work impacted her organization and her team.

Step 3—Help Your Feedback Recipient Take Credit for Success

■ "Oh, it was no big deal. I had a lot of help."

Although just about everyone craves positive reinforcement, it's amazing how many people have trouble accepting it when it's given to them. Many of us were raised with the attitude that accepting a compliment was similar to bragging, or perhaps we just have a hard time believing that we could actually do something right!

Help those you reinforce accept full responsibility for their success.

Help those you reinforce accept full responsibility for their success. While you can acknowledge the contributions of others if your feedback recipient mentions them, emphasize the full importance of your recipient's role:

■ "I realize that the entire team was involved in making the conference a success, but I want especially to thank you for all of your work arranging transportation. Thanks to you, all of the participants arrived in plenty of time to make their presentations."

As the above example illustrates, providing strong examples of the positive effects someone's actions have had within the organization is a good way to help a modest person realize the significance of his or her efforts.

Step 4—Thank and Encourage Your Feedback Recipient

"Thank you" is still one of those magic expressions we love to hear, so be sure to say "thanks" whenever you present reinforcement. Including your thanks toward the end of your reinforcement, after you have described the act and its effect, can be particularly effective because it will be the last thing the employee takes away from the interaction.

As you thank your feedback recipient, encourage him or her to keep up the good work. Make sure your feedback recipient knows that you hope to see the positive behavior or performance repeated in similar situations.

Take a Moment

Think of someone you work with whose positive behavior or performance you would like to reinforce. With that individual in mind, decide what you intend to say at each step of the process.

Describe the behavior or performance you want to reinforce.

_____

_____

Explain the positive impact the behavior or performance has had on the organization.

_____

_____

Help your feedback recipient take responsibility for his or her success.

_____

_____

Thank your feedback recipient for his/her contribution toward meeting individual, group, or organizational goals and encourage similar future behavior or performance.

_____

_____

4

Basic Steps for Giving Redirection

Redirection consists of six basic steps that will help your feedback recipient see the impact of his or her acts and plan for the future:

1. Describe the behavior or performance you want to redirect.

2. Listen to the reaction of your feedback recipient. Your feedback recipient may immediately admit there is a problem and take responsibility for it (Step 4), or you may need to . . .

3. Clarify your expectations for your feedback recipient's behavior or performance. Or explain the negative effect those actions are having on the organization.

4. Help your feedback recipient to acknowledge that a problem exists and take responsibility for it.

5. Develop a plan that will help your feedback recipient adjust his or her actions.

6. Thank your feedback recipient for his or her efforts.

The steps for giving redirection are summarized in the following flowchart.

Steps for Giving Redirection

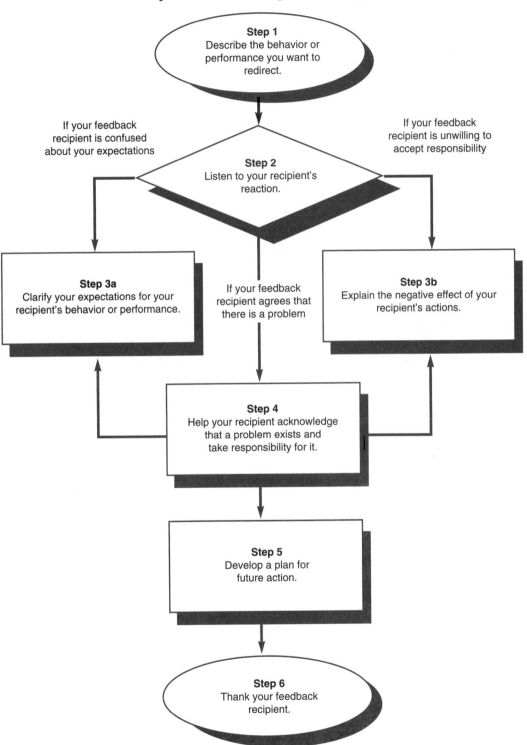

Step 1
Describe the behavior or performance you want to redirect.

If your feedback recipient is confused about your expectations

Step 2
Listen to your recipient's reaction.

If your feedback recipient is unwilling to accept responsibility

Step 3a
Clarify your expectations for your recipient's behavior or performance.

If your feedback recipient agrees that there is a problem

Step 3b
Explain the negative effect of your recipient's actions.

Step 4
Help your recipient acknowledge that a problem exists and take responsibility for it.

Step 5
Develop a plan for future action.

Step 6
Thank your feedback recipient.

4

Step 1—Describe the Behavior or Performance You Want to Redirect

Once again, you should begin the feedback session with a description of the behavior or performance you want to redirect. If the act you are describing is ongoing, try to cite more than one instance of it so that your feedback recipient can get an idea of the extent of the problem, as in these examples:

■ **Behavior in need of redirection:**
"Bob, you were late to work three times this week and twice last week. You were also late five times last month."

■ **Performance in need of redirection:**
"Martha, I found five typing errors in this letter you just finished, and you misspelled the client's name. I also found typing errors in the last two letters you typed for me."

Notice that in both examples, the person giving the feedback simply describes the behavior or performance in question without making a value judgment or expressing anger or disappointment. Beginning your feedback in this way will keep your redirection focused on acts rather than attitudes.

Step 2—Listen to the Reaction of Your Feedback Recipient

Once you have given a detailed description of the behavior or performance you hope to change, give your feedback recipient a chance to respond. Three responses feedback recipients often give include acknowledging the problem, expressing confusion over expectations, or refusing to accept responsibility.

◆ **Acknowledging the problem**
Often, employees are aware of a problem and have been waiting for an opportunity to discuss it:

■ "I know the formatting on the reports has been difficult to read. I've been trying to use the new software, but I just can't figure out how to do it. Can someone show me how?"

If you receive a response like this, it shows that your feedback recipient has taken responsibility for the problem and is ready to correct it. Congratulations—you have completed Step 4! No further discussion of your associate or coworker's actions are necessary: the two of you can immediately begin to develop an action plan to correct the problem as described in Step 5.

4

◆ **Expressing confusion**
Of course, not all feedback sessions will resolve so quickly. Your feedback recipient may respond with confusion regarding your expectations. Perhaps your associate or coworker never understood (or was not given) a clear description of his or her job duties; perhaps expectations for the job have changed over time:

■ "I didn't realize that I was supposed to provide the figures by the beginning of the month—I thought that any time during the first week would be fine."

When you receive a response like this, your next step should be to clarify expectations with your feedback recipient, which we describe in Step 3a.

◆ **Refusing to accept responsibility**
Occasionally your feedback recipient may admit that a problem exists but refuse to take responsibility for it. We've all heard (and possibly given) responses like:

■ "It's not my fault! It's the people in accounting."

■ "I'll try to do better, but you know, there just isn't enough time."

In situations like these, your challenge is to determine whether some outside factor is affecting your feedback recipient's ability to do the job or if he or she is just making excuses. This is especially difficult if your associate or coworker is behaving defensively.

Try to get past your feedback recipient's defensiveness and focus on the content of what he or she is saying.

Try to get past your feedback recipient's defensiveness and focus on the content of what he or she is saying. If there are factors within the organization or work team that are keeping him or her from meeting your expectations, use this time to address them. As your associates and coworkers see that you take their viewpoints seriously, their responses will become less defensive and more cooperative.

Of course, there will also be times when you listen to an associate's or coworker's explanation and determine that you must hold that person responsible for the problem. If your feedback recipient remains defensive, try to focus the conversation on the effects of his or her actions as we discuss in Step 3b—this is your best evidence that a problem exists.

Step 3a—Clarify Your Expectations

If your feedback recipient is surprised or confused by the expectations you and other team members have for his or her performance, take the time to clarify them. This might involve referring back to the original job description or reviewing the directions your recipient has received for performing certain tasks.

As you review your expectations, be sure to give your associate or coworker plenty of opportunity to respond. Be sure that your feedback recipient agrees that the expectations are reasonable; if he or she doesn't, you may need to point out that other people in the organization are working just as hard, or you may need to readjust your expectations in some way. Whatever you negotiate, by the end of this step, you and your feedback recipient should agree on a set of reasonable expectations, and your feedback recipient should be ready to acknowledge his or her responsibility for meeting them. You can develop this further in Step 4.

> **Be sure that your feedback recipient agrees that the expectations are reasonable.**

Step 3b—Explain the Action's Negative Effect

The best way you can help a defensive feedback recipient recognize the need to redirect his or her actions is by giving a thorough description of the effect those actions are having on other members of your team or organization. Again, you should simply state the facts without expressing anger or making a value judgment. Here are examples that illustrate two descriptions we used earlier:

- "When you're late, other employees have to fill in for you until you arrive. Joe had to work overtime twice this week until you arrived, and Sara had to cover for you last week. It isn't fair to the others to expect them to cover for you, and it hurts the quality of our work to keep tired employees on duty after their shift is over."

- "When we send out letters with typing errors, it looks as though we don't care about our clients, especially when we misspell the clients' names. We could lose business if our clients think we don't value them."

Descriptions like these should help your feedback recipient see the impact of his or her behavior or performance and take responsibility for adjusting that action. If your recipient is especially defensive, keep returning to your examples until he or she is ready to accept responsibility and work out a plan to promote change.

4

Step 4—Help Your Recipient Acknowledge That a Problem Exists and Take Responsibility for It

If you can get people to recognize the negative consequences or adverse impact of something they are doing, they will usually agree that it is a problem.

You and the person to whom you are giving feedback cannot collaborate in redirecting behavior or performance until he or she acknowledges that a problem exists and takes responsibility for correcting it. You will know that you have this agreement when you hear your feedback recipient say something like, "Yes, I agree, there is a problem here. What can I do about it?"

If your feedback recipient is slow to acknowledge the problem and accept responsibility, you should continue to present evidence about the extent of the problem until you have agreement. What kind of evidence can you use to convince your recipient that a problem exists and that his or her behavior or performance needs to change?

- ◆ Stress the negative impact that the individual's current performance or behavior is having on coworkers and the organization as a whole.

- ◆ Convince the individual that he or she will face significant consequences if the behavior or performance continues.

If you can get people to recognize the negative consequences or adverse impact of something they are doing, they will usually agree that it is a problem.

Step 5—Develop an Action Plan

The goal of any redirection is improving future performance and behavior. It isn't enough just to point out the need for change to your feedback recipient—you also need to develop a specific plan to help him or her set and meet objectives.

Although you should have some short- and long-term goals in mind before you begin your feedback session, you will want to involve your feedback recipient in the planning process. One way you can do this is by stating an overall goal and then asking for the other person's input on how to meet that goal. Here is an example in which an administrative assistant redirects her manager's difficulty with deadlines:

> **Involve your feedback recipient in the planning process.**

Admin. Asst.:
Ms. Wagner, I really want to get your correspondence typed on time, but I have difficulty when you give me your tapes to transcribe a half hour before the mail has to go out. Is there some way you can give me more time?

Manager:
It's difficult. Those are open cases, and I often don't have the information I need until the last minute.

Admin. Asst.:
Well, could you let me know at the beginning of the day if you think you'll need me to transcribe something? That way I could organize my work so that my last hour is free for your projects.

Manager:
I think I can do that.

Though the administrative assistant might not have gotten as much time for her transcription as she would have liked, she was able to involve her manager in a solution that would help her organize her time effectively, which was her primary objective. When the manager remembers to tell her associate about upcoming transcription, the associate can reinforce that action by saying something like "Thanks for telling me so early. I can get much more done when I have the opportunity to organize my day in advance."

4

Step 6—Thank Your Feedback Recipient for His or Her Efforts

It can be hard to accept redirection. Show your feedback recipient that you appreciate his or her efforts by closing your redirection with a "thank you." This can also be a good time to summarize your conversation and make plans for future meetings:

■ "Thanks for taking the time to talk to me about the sales figures. I really appreciate your willingness to spend an extra day on the road to do follow up, and I want to help you any way I can. Let's get together when you're in the office next week and see how things are going for you."

Staying on Track

Don't allow yourself to get distracted in the course of a feedback session.

These steps for giving reinforcement and redirection will allow you to give useful, supportive feedback that focuses on acts rather than attitudes. Following these steps should get you through even a potentially difficult feedback situation with a minimum of stress. But the steps can help you only if you follow them. Don't allow yourself to get distracted in the course of a feedback session. Even if your feedback recipient tries to steer the conversation onto other topics or becomes argumentative, focus on the steps. They will give your feedback session direction and ensure that you provide your recipient with as much useful information as possible.

Take a Moment

Think of someone you work with whose behavior or performance you would like to redirect. With that individual in mind, decide what you intend to say at each step of the process.

Describe the behavior or performance you want to redirect.

_____

_____

Imagine what you think that person's response will be.

_____

_____

Clarify your expectations for your feedback receiver OR explain the negative effect the behavior or performance has had on the organization and help your receiver take responsibility for his or her actions.

_____

_____

Help your recipient to acknowledge that a problem exists and take responsibility for it.

_____

_____

Develop a plan that will help the receiver of your feedback adjust his or her actions.

_____

_____

Thank your feedback recipient.

_____

_____

Documenting Your Feedback

Too often we're so busy handling day-to-day worries that we forget to make note of the positive things we encounter. If you have given an associate or coworker reinforcement on a significant achievement or project, don't forget to document your feedback for that individual's personnel file. Making a record of your positive assessment will help that employee receive the rewards and recognition he or she deserves when performance is reviewed.

You should also make note of any redirection that you give. Even if you do not think that the problem is serious enough to include in the employee's personnel file, keep a record of the redirection for yourself. Include the types of details we discussed in Chapter 3—these are the key elements of good documentation:

◆ What happened?

◆ Where and when did it occur?

◆ Who was involved?

◆ How did it affect others?

If the receiver of your feedback successfully redirects his or her performance, you will have a record of the feedback process that will help you track the employee's success. And, in the unfortunate event that the employee does not respond to redirection and the problem becomes worse, you will have documentation that you attempted to deal with it. This could be significant if the problem becomes so serious that the employee must be disciplined or terminated.

Providing Higher Levels of Information

In Chapter 2, we discussed the process of specifying—providing more and more specific, detailed information to your feedback recipient. Following the steps for providing reinforcement or redirection that we've outlined here will help you provide the detailed information your feedback receiver needs to meet individual, group, and organizational goals, as illustrated in Diagram 3. Beginning with your description of the act in question, each step of the feedback process provides further details that can help your feedback recipient improve his or her performance or behavior.

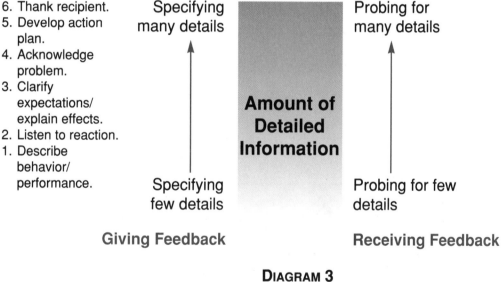

ACHIEVING GOALS

6. Thank recipient.
5. Develop action plan.
4. Acknowledge problem.
3. Clarify expectations/ explain effects.
2. Listen to reaction.
1. Describe behavior/ performance.

Specifying many details

↑

Specifying few details

Amount of Detailed Information

Probing for many details

↑

Probing for few details

Giving Feedback   **Receiving Feedback**

DIAGRAM 3

Self-Check: Chapter 4 Review

Suggested answers appear on pages 100 and 101.

1. True or False?
   There is no need to worry about scheduling an appropriate time for giving feedback. You can provide redirection and reinforcement anytime, anywhere.

2. True or False?
   It is perfectly all right to redirect an individual employee in the presence of other employees.

3. List the four basic steps for providing reinforcement.

   a. _____

   b. _____

   c. _____

   d. _____

4. List the six basic steps for providing redirection.

   a. _____

   b. _____

   c. _____

   d. _____

   e. _____

   f. _____

5. True or False?
   It is important to document both reinforcement and redirection.

Chapter *Five*

Steps for Receiving Feedback Effectively

Chapter Objectives

▶ Follow the basic steps for receiving reinforcement or redirection of your job performance and job-related behavior.

▶ Probe for more information when receiving redirection or reinforcement.

▶ Understand how the amount of information you receive can help you achieve individual, group, and organizational goals.

How Do You React to Feedback?

Think about the last time you received feedback from someone. What did you do? Did you listen to the feedback and try to learn as much as you could from it? Did you ask questions in order to receive as much detailed information as possible? Or did you become defensive?

If you spend all your time explaining yourself, you won't have time to really hear what the person giving redirection is trying to say.

It's always tempting to make excuses whenever we receive redirection. After all, you probably had very good reasons for approaching your work in the way you did, and it's natural to want to explain those reasons. But if you spend all your time explaining yourself, you won't have time to really hear what the person giving redirection is trying to say—that your actions are creating some negative effects for your organization and need to be changed. You must put aside your feelings of defensiveness in order to be able to focus on the details that can help you change your behavior or performance.

You can make the same kind of mistake when you receive reinforcement. If someone compliments your work, you may want to stop right there and enjoy the praise without asking for further details, or, if you're a modest person, you may want to deny the praise completely. But you won't benefit from either approach. The only way you will be able to repeat your actions and develop them further is by probing for specific details about what aspects of your behavior or performance have had the most positive effects and how you should repeat them.

Take a Moment

Think about the last time you received feedback from someone. What did you do?

_____

_____

Was your reaction in that instance typical of how you react when receiving feedback? Check those that apply. Did you tend to:

_____ Get defensive and try to explain your actions?

_____ Find someone with whom to share all or part of the blame for the problem?

_____ Shut down and not listen, focusing instead on what you can do to regain favor in the other person's eyes?

_____ Listen carefully to what the person is saying so you can understand and probe for more information if necessary?

5

Listening and Learning from Feedback

You'll get the most from reinforcement and redirection if you make the commitment to listen and learn in all feedback situations. You can evaluate reinforcement and redirection most effectively if you develop these habits for receiving feedback:

◆ Become a careful listener.

◆ Keep all feedback in perspective.

◆ Try to learn from all feedback, even feedback that is presented poorly.

Become a Careful Listener

The first thing you can do to get the most from every feedback session is to develop effective listening skills.

The first thing you can do to get the most from every feedback session is to develop effective listening skills. Listening is probably the most important communication skill we can develop, yet few of us know how to listen effectively. How many times have you found your mind wandering when someone was talking to you? Any distracting thoughts can keep a person from being an effective listener—an impending deadline, rumors about corporate layoffs—even worries about a child's Little League game.

It's especially easy for us to become distracted when we are receiving feedback. We not only listen with all of the other concerns that generally crowd our minds for attention, but we may also be trying to generate excuses for our acts even as they are being described to us.

Try to enter every feedback situation with the attitude that you will concentrate on what the person giving feedback is saying. Don't try to generate responses as the person is talking, just listen. If the person's perspective seems strange to you, ask yourself why he or she might see things in that way. You will likely have plenty of time to present your own observations after he or she is done talking.

Keep Feedback in Perspective

It's easy to overreact to feedback. If someone reinforces a positive behavior or a successful performance, it's natural to enjoy the positive feelings of knowing that we have done our job well. But if we extend that positive reaction to the point that we believe we can do no wrong, we are taking an unrealistic view of our own abilities.

The same thing can happen when we receive redirection, especially if that redirection is given in an inappropriate or overly critical manner. (Remember, not everyone has the expertise you will be able to demonstrate when you complete this book.) By dwelling on the negative, you can turn a simple comment on one specific act into a criticism of your entire job performance— or even your life!

Remember to keep all feedback in perspective. Use feedback as a guide to determine if you should repeat or change specific actions, not as something to dwell on.

It's easy to overreact to feedback.

5

Try to Learn from All Feedback

In a perfect world, all of the feedback we receive would be presented in an appropriate manner. If your organization is encouraging all of its members to give each other useful, ongoing feedback, this is certainly the goal. However, human beings aren't perfect, and feedback is sometimes given poorly even in the most well-intentioned organizations. It's tempting to write off inappropriate feedback as rude and obnoxious, but by doing so you may miss out on important information that can help you do your job better.

As you become more experienced in receiving feedback effectively, you will be able to exert some control in situations in which feedback is given to you ineffectively. By asking appropriate questions, you can salvage many feedback situations that get off on the wrong foot and gain valuable information in the process. You will also help other team members to develop effective feedback skills by modeling those skills and encouraging them to do so in return.

Attempt to learn something from all feedback you receive.

Make a commitment to attempt to learn something from all feedback you receive, even in situations that initially seem unpleasant.

Are You Ready for Feedback?

If you've made the commitment to listen to both redirection and reinforcement with an open mind and to avoid denying or making excuses for what you hear, you're ready for your next feedback session. You can begin by helping to choose the time and place.

Helping Choose the Appropriate Time and Place

Has the person giving you feedback asked for your help in choosing an appropriate time and place? If so, help him or her create a situation in which neither of you will be distracted or uncomfortable.

If you find yourself in a situation in which a person begins to give you feedback in an inappropriate setting—providing redirection in a busy hallway or in front of a group of coworkers, for example—politely ask if you can move the discussion to another time and place where you can give it your full attention. Remember, feedback should never be used as a means to belittle employees in front of others. If you find yourself in a situation in which you believe this is happening, you are perfectly within your rights to ask that the topic be taken up in another setting.

Staying Calm and Cordial

Approach every feedback situation with confidence, knowing that the information you receive will help you improve your performance and move closer toward your goals. Resolve to stay calm throughout every feedback session. Use a pleasant tone of voice and maintain eye contact throughout the interaction. Even if the person giving feedback becomes unpleasant, it doesn't help the situation if you raise your voice.

Approach every feedback situation with confidence.

Don't Be Afraid to Ask Questions

The more detailed information you receive in the course of a feedback session, the more that feedback session will benefit you. And the way to guarantee that you receive redirection or reinforcement you can use is to ask questions—to probe for more and more details—and to be sure you understand those details.

5

Basic Steps for Receiving Feedback

The process of probing for information can be easy if you follow these steps:

- ◆ Ask for as much detailed information as possible.

- ◆ Paraphrase what you think you've heard.

- ◆ Seek suggestions for future action.

- ◆ Thank the person giving the feedback.

The steps for receiving feedback are summarized in the following flowchart.

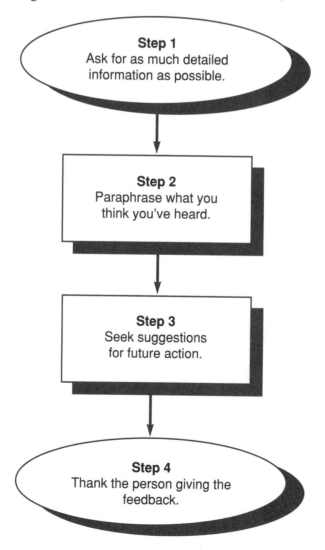

Step 1
Ask for as much detailed information as possible.

Step 2
Paraphrase what you think you've heard.

Step 3
Seek suggestions for future action.

Step 4
Thank the person giving the feedback.

Step 1—Ask for Details

Whether you are receiving reinforcement or redirection, it's important to probe for as many details as possible. Sometimes probing may be as easy as thanking someone for a compliment:

- "I'm so glad you liked the work I did on the Gleason contract. If you tell me specifically what it was you liked about it, I'll be able to do it again on the next one."

In cases of redirection, probing may be a bit more difficult. You may not be eager to ask for examples of ways in which your actions have negatively impacted others. But it is worth the effort to probe for as many details as you can get—they are the tools you can use to improve your performance and meet your goals. If the person you are addressing is skilled at giving feedback, you'll find it easy to get as much information as you need:

Manager:
I never realized that my instructions to the word-processing department weren't clear. What information do you need from me that I'm not giving you?

Typist:
We really need you to tell us exactly when you need your project done instead of just saying "sometime soon," and we also need to know how many copies you want made for your files.

Asking for more information is useful even when the person giving you feedback is not skilled at expressing him–or herself. Believe it or not, requesting details is one of the best ways to handle inappropriate feedback.

5

Requesting details is one of the best ways to handle inappropriate feedback.

Consider this example:

Editor:
I don't know what the matter is with you people. Can't you do a simple layout?

Designer:
I'm sorry you don't like this layout. Can you tell us what it is you don't like about it?

Editor:
Well, it's awful, that's all.

Designer:
Let's start from the beginning. Is it the headline you don't like?

Editor:
No, that's all right. It's the rest of it.

Designer:
How about the typeface? Is that what's bothering you?

Editor:
No, that's not it either. It's just too crowded—it looks all jumbled.

Designer:
So you think it needs more white space?

Editor:
Yes, that's it, white space.

Obviously, the editor in this example was not giving effective feedback, which forced the designer to work twice as hard to learn what was wrong with the layout. The designer could easily have become frustrated with the editor, and the entire feedback session could have ended as a nasty argument. But by staying cool and asking for details, the designer was able to learn exactly what was bothering the editor and can now use that information when preparing other layouts. Though the designer had to work a little to get the necessary information, the information gained will be worth the effort.

If you work with someone who frequently gives you inappropriate feedback, you should consider giving that person some redirection on the way he or she is interacting with you. It is possible to comment on the way another person gives feedback in a way that is constructive and nonthreatening. The designer in the first example might tell the editor something like this:

■ "I want to design layouts we can both be proud of, but I can't really make the changes you want when your comments are so general. I think it would help both of us work better together if you would refer to specific parts of the layout when you want me to make changes."

Step 2—Paraphrase What You Think You Heard

Even with careful listening, you might miss some of the details of the feedback being presented to you. It's easy to focus in on just one aspect of another's feedback and ignore the rest, especially if you are having a strong emotional reaction to what's being said. Paraphrasing your understanding of the feedback is a good way to make sure that your interpretation matches the intention of the person giving the feedback.

Wait until the other person has finished describing his or her perspective on the situation before you begin to paraphrase. Then simply restate your understanding of the feedback in your own words and ask the person giving the feedback if that interpretation is correct. Give the other person a chance to respond to your paraphrase and add any additional information, as in this example:

■ "So, what I hear you saying is that I need to spend a little more time with our clients during their initial visits."

"That's right. They need to have a chance to get to know you and feel comfortable before we start working on their accounts."

5

> Paraphrasing your understanding of the feedback is a good way to make sure that your interpretation matches the intention of the person giving the feedback.

Step 3—Seek Suggestions for Future Action

Whether you're receiving reinforcement or redirection, feedback should never be a means to dwell on past performance. The purpose of feedback is to share information that will help you plan for the future.

> **Always be sure that future plans are discussed in the course of any feedback session.**

Always be sure that future plans are discussed in the course of any feedback session. If you are receiving reinforcement, clarify exactly which acts should be repeated and when you should repeat them:

■ "I'm glad you like the way I handled the presentation in this morning's meeting. If you could tell me what you think were the strongest points, I'll be sure to do something similar in my next presentation."

If you are receiving redirection, ask the other person to help you develop a plan for changing your future actions.

■ "I realize I lost my temper when that customer complained last week. I really don't know how to deal with customers when they get so irate. Do you have any suggestions?"

Never leave a feedback session until both you and the person giving the feedback have agreed on a future course of action.

Step 4—Thank the Person Giving the Feedback

It takes courage to give another person direct, honest feedback. Show the other person that you value the effort he or she made, as well as the time it took to prepare and present the feedback, by saying "Thank you" at the end of any feedback session.

Though you may find it difficult, it's especially important to thank someone who has given you feedback in an ineffective way—especially since you have likely been able to turn the interaction in to a positive one by probing for useful information. Your handling of the situation has given that person the opportunity to learn more effective feedback techniques by observing how you probed for information. Saying "thanks" demonstrates that your behavior always remains professional and sets a positive tone for your next interaction.

Take a Moment

Think of the last time someone gave you feedback that was lacking in specific details. What was the essence of the feedback you got?

_____

_____

What could you have said to that individual to probe for more information?

1. What details might you have asked for?

   _____

2. How might you have paraphrased his or her words?

   _____

3. How might you have sought suggestions for future action?

   _____

4. What could you have said to sincerely thank the person giving the feedback?

   _____

5

Probing for Higher Levels of Information

In Chapter 4, we saw how, through the process of specifying, a person giving feedback can provide increasing amounts of information that will help the feedback receiver achieve his or her goals. The process of probing has the same effect.

As the person receiving feedback follows the steps of asking for information, paraphrasing that information, and seeking suggestions for future action, he or she receives more and more specific details about job performance, as illustrated in Diagram 4. The more details you are able to receive from a feedback situation, the more tools you have to help you achieve greater and greater success.

By following the steps for giving and receiving feedback effectively, you and your coworkers can share information about job performance and behaviors easily. In our next chapter, you will have to chance to see what role your individual communication style plays in the feedback process.

ACHIEVING GOALS

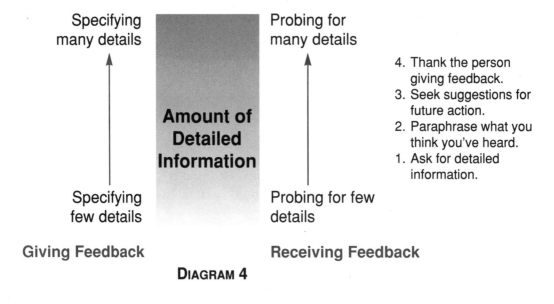

DIAGRAM 4

Self-Check: Chapter 5 Review

Suggested answers appear on page 101.

1. True or False?
   With the right attitude, you can learn from any feedback situation, even one that begins inappropriately.

2. True or False?
   You should try to keep all feedback in perspective; don't allow the redirection of one act to cause you to question your entire job performance.

3. True or False?
   If a person begins to give you feedback at an inappropriate time and place, you should politely ask him or her if you can find a better setting where neither of you will be distracted.

4. True or False?
   Eye contact with the person giving you feedback really isn't important. If you feel uncomfortable during a feedback session, just look at the floor.

5. List the four basic steps for effectively receiving feedback.

   a._____

   b. _____

   c. _____

   d. _____

6. True or False?
   Remaining calm and asking for further details is an effective way to deal with someone who is giving you inappropriate feedback.

7. True or False?
   Always remember to thank a person who has just given you feedback, even if the interaction started off on the wrong foot.

Chapter *Six*

Feedback and Communication Styles

Chapter Objectives

▶ Identify your preferred communication style.

▶ Recognize the impact your preferred communication style has on the way you tend to give and receive feedback.

▶ Understand other styles of communication and how those styles relate to feedback.

▶ Adapt your communication style to the needs of the feedback situation, particularly the needs of feedback recipients.

What Are Communication Styles?

All of us have developed communication patterns that reflect our individual identities.

Communication styles play an important part in the giving and receiving of feedback. All of us have developed communication patterns that reflect our individual identities. These patterns develop over time and become our preferred manner of communicating.

Your effectiveness in giving and receiving feedback will be enhanced if you are aware of your preferred communication style and that of your feedback recipient. By recognizing the strengths and weaknesses of both styles, you can more easily adjust your style to avoid conflicts and ensure understanding.

There are four major communication styles:

◆ **Driver**—The driver is direct and task-oriented.

◆ **Collaborator**—The collaborator is enthusiastic and relationship-oriented.

- **Contributor**—The contributor is supportive and avoids change and confrontation.

- **Investigator**—The investigator is accurate and detail-oriented.

Though our individual communication styles are usually a composite of all four styles, we tend to have one stronger, preferred style. The chart below describes some of the strengths and potential stumbling blocks associated with the four styles. Which style comes closest to describing the way you tend to communicate?

Communication Style	Strengths	Potential Stumbling Blocks
Driver	Direct	Challenges others
	Practical	Impatient
	Decisive	Insensitive
	Confident	Overly independent
	Clear, to the point	Need for control, domineering
	Task-oriented	
Collaborator	Talkative	Overly sensitive
	Friendly	Lack of follow-through/details
	Enthusiastic	Unprepared, disorganized
	Approachable, open	Subjective in decision-making
	Initiates through involvement of others	
Contributor	Supportive, patient	Avoids confrontation, passive
	Predictable	Slow to change
	Easygoing, calm	Slow to initiate
	Listens actively	Indecisive
	Responsive to others	Withholds feelings
Investigator	Accurate, well-prepared	Too critical, insensitive
	Diplomatic	Inflexible
	Analytical	Withdrawn
	Cautious, restrained	Overly cautious
	Systematic, detail-oriented	Imposes high standards

6

Most of us give
and receive
feedback in
a manner
consistent with
our dominant
communication
style.

How Styles Affect Feedback

Most of us give and receive feedback in a manner consistent with our dominant communication style. Review the preferred manner for giving and receiving feedback for each of the four styles, paying particular attention to your own style.

Communication Style	Prefers to Give/Receive Feedback
Driver	Quickly
	Directly
	To the point
	Focusing on the "WHATs"
Collaborator	Conversationally
	Allowing time for anecdotal support
	Sensitively
	Allowing time for much verbalizing
	Focusing on the "WHATs"
Contributor	Patient, allowing time to respond
	Nonthreateningly
	Clearly
	Supportively
	Privately
	Focusing on "WHATs" and "HOWs"
Investigator	Objectively
	Thoroughly
	Accurately
	Patiently, allowing time to change
	With no surprises
	Focusing on "WHATs" and "WHYs"

Understanding the Communication Styles of Others

Knowing and understanding your preferred communication style is important because in order to fully appreciate others' styles, you must first appreciate your own. You will want to be conscious of your own communication preferences when giving and receiving feedback from others. But your primary focus needs to be on what you believe the other person's preferences are.[1]

If you are giving feedback to a coworker or an associate, you need to be sensitive to that person's communication style. By matching that individual's style, or delivering your feedback in a way that is comfortable to the person, he or she will be more likely to hear what you have to say and to be open to changing his or her behavior or improving performance.

When receiving feedback from others, be aware of their preferred communication styles. Understanding their styles explains their approach in giving you their feedback. Understanding their approach enables you to get beyond "how" they are giving you the feedback and allows you to concentrate instead on probing for specifics (the "whats" and "whys").

6

Let's look at an example of a supervisor with a Driver communication style redirecting the performance of an associate with an Investigator style. Note how the supervisor adapts the basic steps for giving redirection to a style that is compatible with her associate's style, not necessarily her own. She enters the feedback discussion well prepared, ready to provide lots of facts and specific details. She knows her associate is going to want to know "why" he needs to improve his performance, not just "what" she sees as unsatisfactory performance.

---

[1] The concept of communication styles is certainly not unique to this book. Several organizations also offer assessment tools for determining communication styles.

Driver Giving Redirection to an Investigator

◆ **Step 1**—Describe the behavior or performance you want to redirect.

Sharon:
Bill, we need to talk about your follow-through on the customer inquiries assigned to you in the database. Of the 49 inquiries—all five weeks old or older—21 are at a Stage 3 or higher in reaching resolution. That means 28—or over 50 percent—have had initial contact but little follow-up.

◆ **Step 2**—Listen to the reaction of your feedback recipient.

If Bill acknowledges that he has not consistently followed through on customer inquiries and that this is a problem, Sharon can move immediately to Step 5 and help Bill develop an action plan. Otherwise, Sharon must take the time to help Bill understand and acknowledge the impact his performance is having on others. Until Bill recognizes the consequences of his performance and takes responsibility for them, there's little incentive for him to change.

◆ **Step 3**—Explain the effect the behavior/ performance is having on the organization.

Sharon:
When you are slow in reaching resolution on inquiries, it has far-reaching effects. For example, until an inquiry reaches Stage 4, the fulfillment department can't access it and begin preparations for processing. This causes a backlog online and makes it difficult for fulfillment to schedule employees.

We know that delays in follow-through result in fewer sales. We need to be responsive to customer inquiries while their interest is strong. Delays result in lower commissions for you, missed sales targets for our team, and less revenue for the company.

◆ **Step 4**—Help your feedback recipient acknowledge that a problem exists and take responsibility for it.

Sharon should continue to discuss the situation with Bill until he acknowledges his responsibility for the situation:

Bill:
I can see that I need to move more quickly if I want to meet our sales goals. Let's set up a timetable.

◆ **Step 5**—Develop a plan that will help the receiver of your feedback adjust his or her actions.

Sharon:
Bill, in order to meet our goals, we need to reach resolution on all inquiries within eight weeks of the inquiry date. What can you do, and how can I help, to increase your rate of follow-through?

Bill and Sharon can now work together to set short- and long-term goals for Bill's performance and create an action plan that will help Bill meet those goals.

◆ **Step 6**—Thank your feedback recipient for his or her efforts.

After they've made specific plans, Sharon can thank Bill, review their conversation, and arrange a future meeting:

6

Sharon:
Bill, thanks for taking the time for this talk. You've acknowledged that your delays in reaching resolution are having negative effects, and you've identified several steps that will help you reach resolution more quickly. I'm here to help you if you need it. Let's get together again next Tuesday and assess the progress you've made.

Take a Moment

How well did Sharon (a Driver) do in matching the way she provided feedback to Bill (an Investigator)?

Was she well prepared? _____ yes _____ no

Was she thorough? _____ yes _____ no

Did she explain the "whys"
for improving? _____ yes _____ no

Was she objective and
nonaccusatory? _____ yes _____ no

Was she detailed and specific
in her examples? _____ yes _____ no

Being aware of the four communication styles and adjusting your feedback to the style of the person to whom you are speaking can help you give and receive feedback more effectively. In the next chapter, you will have the chance to assess your current level of feedback skills and create an action plan for developing them further.

Self-Check: Chapter 6 Review

Suggested answers appear on page 101.

Match each communication style with the appropriate description.

_____ 1. collaborator   a. detail-oriented, accurate

_____ 2. investigator   b. direct, task-oriented

_____ 3. contributor   c. supportive, avoids change and confrontation

_____ 4. driver   d. relationship-oriented, enthusiastic

Complete each sentence.

5. In order to fully appreciate others' communication styles, you must first understand and appreciate

_____

_____

6

6. Whether you are giving or receiving feedback, it is important to be aware of, and in some cases match,

_____

_____

Chapter *Seven*

Handling Difficult Feedback Situations

Chapter Objectives

▶ Recognize some typical situations in which giving and receiving feedback may be difficult.

▶ Use the basic steps for effectively giving and receiving feedback to handle difficult situations.

Identifying Difficult Feedback Situations

Let's face it, some feedback situations can be especially difficult. Providing redirection to someone with a "difficult" personality or accepting redirection from someone who speaks in vague generalities can leave you feeling frustrated and demoralized.

But difficult feedback situations can end positively. You can take control of even the most unpleasant, awkward feedback situations by following the basic steps discussed in this book. You will want to review those steps when you face situations such as:

◆ Redirecting an employee whose performance problems are compounded by personal problems, such as a recent divorce or financial difficulties.

◆ Redirecting employees with difficult personalities.

◆ Redirecting a coworker whose work habits disturb you.

◆ Receiving redirection from someone who uses such broad generalities that you can't figure out what the issue is.

When Personal Problems Affect Performance

It may be awkward to redirect an employee whom you know is having personal problems, but accepting poor performance doesn't help that employee or your organization. Because your feedback recipient is under stress, be prepared for some atypical responses, such as crying or blaming. Emphasize that you are not trying to create more stress for your recipient; you only want to help that person perform his or her job. Although you and other team members should not take on too much of your feedback recipient's workload, you can discuss ways you and the team can help resolve the problem when you create the action plan:

◆ **Step 1**—Describe the behavior or performance you want to redirect.

Manager:
Jared, several clients have indicated that you haven't returned their voice mail messages. We really put a priority on returning calls; is something keeping you from doing this?

◆ **Step 2**—Listen to your recipient's reaction.

Jared:
I've been finding it difficult to focus because I'm getting a divorce and our child custody hearing is next week. I just don't see how you can expect me to concentrate until this is all over.

◆ **Step 3:**—Explain the negative effect of your recipient's actions.

Manager:
Our company prides itself on returning client calls within 24 hours. When you don't return calls within that time frame, your calls end up on a list for redistribution to other team members. Several of them have complained about the length of the redistribution list. This not only has a negative effect on morale, but it also weakens our service to our clients. I really think we have a problem here. Do you?

7

◆ Step 4—Help your recipient acknowledge that a problem exists and take responsibility for it.

Jared:
I would think you could be a little more understanding at a time like this. I promise you as soon as this whole mess is over, I'll be on top of things again.

Obviously, the feedback recipient is not ready to acknowledge, or does not yet understand, that a problem exists and he has responsibility for correcting it. At this point, the person giving the feedback needs to point out the consequences of allowing the problem to continue.

Manager:
Everybody on your team is already working at top capacity, and it's unfair to ask them to carry part of your responsibility. We need you to return all of your own client calls within 24 hours starting today, or I'll have to take disciplinary action.

Jared:
Could this affect my pay increase that's scheduled to begin next month?

Manager:
Yes, it could. Do you agree that we have a problem?

Jared:
Well, yes, I guess we do have a problem. I need that additional money to cover child support.

◆ Step 5—Develop a plan for future action.

Manager:
All right then, I'd suggest that starting today you keep up with all client calls and return all of them within 24 hours.

◆ Step 6—Thank your feedback recipient.

Manager:
Thank you, Jared. I realize that you're dealing with a lot right now, which makes it all the more important to maintain a good performance record at work.

When Personalities Clash

We've all met people with difficult personalities. Some seem to become angry at the slightest provocation. They get away with a lot because no one wants to say or do anything that will set them off. Others appear to have no reaction whatsoever. You may find yourself wondering if they've heard a thing you've said.

People like these can be a challenge to work with in the best of circumstances; if you have had unpleasant interactions with them in the past, you may be especially reluctant to give them redirection. But remember, following the basic steps can help you reach even the most difficult personality.

It can be especially challenging to redirect a noncommunicative person who finds it difficult to engage in dialogue. Your goal is to get the person to admit that a problem exists and take an active role in developing the action plan to solve it. Once you've described the problem, you may need to wait a while for this person's reaction (Step 2). Be patient. Let the other person see that you will not leave without some type of response:

■ "So, do you understand what the situation is?"

"Yes, I guess so."

"How would you describe it, then? In your own words—"

Once you are satisfied that a noncommunicative person truly understands the nature of a problem and acknowledges responsibility for it (Step 4), you can begin to involve him or her in developing an action plan for its solution (Step 5). Again, you will have to be patient and ask questions to be sure the individual understands exactly what steps he or she should take to improve behavior or performance.

7

On the opposite end of the communication spectrum, people who habitually overreact may cry, yell, or become defensive in response to your redirection. Don't let them use this behavior to take control of the situation. Remain calm and continue to focus on the steps until they acknowledge their role in the problem, even if a recipient's reaction attacks you personally:

■ "You've had it in for me ever since I joined this company. This is just another of your attempts to get rid of me."

"We're talking about specific behaviors you demonstrate when working with other team members, not about whether anyone is out to get you. When you miss key deadlines, don't answer your E-mail, and interrupt others during meetings, you make it difficult for the teams you are part of to meet their goals. Do you understand why others perceive you as being uncooperative?"

When a Coworker's Personal Habits Affect Your Work

It may seem trivial, but sometimes people's work habits and personal grooming can affect others in their work environment. Some of the most common problems of this type involve:

♦ Loud gum chewing.

♦ Dirty coffee mugs left in others' offices or common areas.

♦ Bad breath, body odor, or strong perfume.

♦ Incessant personal phone calls.

♦ Sloppy or inappropriate dress.

One of the most difficult things you will ever have to do is to tell another person that his or her body odor or perfume is overpowering. However, you may need to provide this very personal kind of feedback if the problem is affecting your ability to do your job. Remember that you are doing the other person, yourself, and everyone else in the work area a favor, although it will be difficult to keep that in perspective at the time.

Don't feel the need to develop this type of redirection to the same extent that you do others. You do not need to get your feedback recipient to acknowledge responsibility for the problem or develop an action plan. Simply state your feedback in the most polite way you can and allow the other person to deal with it privately:

- ■ "I really like your perfume, but because we have to work together so closely, there are days when it gets a little strong for me. I've been wondering if you could wear a little less of it."

Because these problems are so personal, you should present this type of redirection in a private setting where your conversation cannot be overheard. Some feedback recipients may become defensive or display hurt feelings; others will want to talk about the problem. Every situation is different—just try to approach each sensitively. You might ask yourself if the feedback recipient would feel more comfortable if he or she received this information from someone of the same sex. You should also present this type of feedback as your own reaction. Don't say something like "everybody's been complaining." This will only make your feedback recipient feel that he or she has been the focus of office jokes.

7

When You Receive Overly General Redirection

No matter how awkward or unpleasant a feedback situation may appear at first, you can take control and turn it into something positive.

It's difficult to remember that all feedback can be valuable when you receive redirection that is vague and unfocused. But remember, no matter how badly a feedback situation starts out, you can derive some benefit from it by asking the right questions, as these members of a retail sales team discover in a meeting with their manager:

Manager:
Your performance last weekend was terrible. I wish I could apologize to every customer who came in this store. I don't know how I'm going to explain this to headquarters.

Associate 1:
Excuse me. I can see you're upset, but could you please explain what exactly you're upset about?

Manager:
What do you mean, what am I upset about? Saturday was terrible.

Associate 2:
But what was terrible about it? Were our sales figures down?

Manager:
No, they were better than average.

Associate 3:
Did our shelf stock run low?

Manager:
No, that was fine. It was the lines.

Associate 3:
You mean our register lines? I thought those ran smoothly.

Manager:
Smoothly! You had lines of customers strung across the store during the noon hour.

Associate 1:
I'm sorry. We got our lunch breaks confused and were shorthanded for a little while.

Manager:
Well, why don't you post a sign-up sheet so that you can see who goes when?

Associate 2:
That's a very good idea. We'll do that today.

Taking Control of the Situation

These are just a few of the difficult feedback situations you might encounter on the job—you have probably encountered many others! But remember, no matter how awkward or unpleasant a feedback situation may appear at first, you can take control and turn it into something positive.

7

Chapter *Eight*

Developing Your Feedback Skills

Chapter Objectives

▶ Reassess your current feedback skills.

▶ Create an action plan for improving your feedback skills.

Reassessing Your Feedback Skills

At the beginning of this book, you had the opportunity to assess your current feedback skills. Now it's time to develop an action plan for improving those areas in which you were weak.

The following statements represent feedback skills that you have learned about in this book. Mark each statement that you would like to incorporate into your personal action plan.

Skills for Giving Effective Feedback

_____ I will pick an appropriate time and place to give feedback.

_____ I will keep my emotions in check, remain calm, and keep my voice even.

_____ I will provide specific, detailed information about the employee's behavior or performance.

_____ I will explain the impact the employee's actions are having on the team or organization.

_____ I will really listen to the responses of those receiving my feedback.

_____ I will clarify my expectations if there is any confusion about the action in question.

_____ I will remember to thank and encourage the receivers of my feedback.

_____ I will provide input as needed in developing an action plan for meeting behavioral or performance goals.

_____ I will focus on the steps of the feedback process to keep the dialogue on track.

_____ I will try to understand feedback from the other person's point of view and preferred communication style.

8

Skills for Receiving Feedback Effectively

_____ I will truly listen to what feedback givers are saying.

_____ I will keep feedback in perspective and won't overreact.

_____ I will try to learn from all feedback, even if it's given poorly.

_____ I will admit to and learn from questions about my performance or behavior at work.

_____ I will attempt to turn every feedback session into a useful encounter.

_____ I will accept redirection and reinforcement rather than denying them.

_____ I will accept responsibility for my role in achieving individual, team, and organizational goals.

_____ I will accept responsibility for developing solutions to performance and behavioral problems that threaten goals.

_____ I will accept responsibility for keeping my emotions in check during feedback discussions.

_____ I will listen and learn in all feedback situations.

Developing an Action Plan

Take some time now to develop an action plan for improving those skills that you checked. There are any number of ways that you can develop your skills at giving and receiving feedback. Here are a few you might try:

◆ Identify another person in your organization who you believe gives and receives feedback effectively and observe that person. Take note of the things that person does that makes his or her feedback effective. Then try to develop those actions yourself.

◆ Is there a person in your organization to whom you frequently give feedback? Ask that person to rate your skills. Do you give that person enough information so that he or she can effectively improve behavior and performance, or is that person often confused by your feedback? Based on that person's response, determine which feedback skills you need to improve.

◆ Is there a person in your organization who frequently gives you feedback? Do you accept that person's feedback with an open mind, or do you become defensive and make excuses? Ask that person to rate your skills as a feedback recipient, and determine if there are things you can do to improve those skills.

◆ Talk to someone in your organization who deals with feedback situations effectively, and ask that person to be your mentor. You might try role-playing feedback situations with that person so that you can practice both giving and receiving feedback in a comfortable environment.

◆ Learn more about feedback and communication skills. American Media has a number of excellent books and videos that can help you.

◆ Practice your feedback skills whenever possible. Don't shy away from the need to respond to another employee's behavior or performance, and encourage your associates and coworkers to do the same for you.

8

97

As you consider these options, choose two or three that you would like to try and create an action plan for following through on them in the next few weeks. Your plan could look something like this:

Feedback Action Plan:

- Ask the new sales trainee if I have been giving her useful feedback about her customer service skills. Ask her if there are different types of information I haven't been giving her that she would find useful.

- Observe how the district sales manager gives me feedback during our next review. Make note of techniques that I like and don't like and compare them to the way I give feedback to my associates.

- Ask Richard to help me role-play a redirection session. Ask him to pretend to be defensive so I can practice dealing with excuses.

Take the self-assessments at the beginning of this book again after you've had a few months to develop your skills, and see if you score differently. With a little practice, you'll soon be able to give your associates, coworkers, and supervisors useful feedback, and you'll be able to effectively receive feedback that will help you achieve your own professional goals.

Chapter 1 Review (page 21)

1. Their job performance and work-related behavior
2. Silence, criticism, and praise
3. Redirection and reinforcement
4. Effective feedback is focused on acts, directed toward the future, goal oriented, multidirectional, supportive, and ongoing (choose any three).

Chapter 2 Review (page 30)

1. Detailed feedback is specific, accurate, and inquiring.
2. As close as possible to the time the act in question occurred.
3. Specifying
4. Probing

Chapter 3 Review (page 41)

1. True
2. False—Your feedback recipient needs detailed feedback in order to know which actions to repeat and which to change.
3. True
4. True
5. False—It is always easier to give redirection or reinforcement when the action in question is fresh in everyone's mind.

Chapter 4 Review (page 62)

1. False—You should try to identify a time when you and your feedback recipient can speak privately without being interrupted. Try to choose a time when neither of you will be overly tired or stressed.
2. False—Redirection in front of a group will only embarrass your feedback recipient and create hostility.
3. a. Describe the behavior or performance you want to reinforce.
   b. Explain the positive impact that act has had on the organization.
   c. Help the receiver of your feedback take credit for his or her success.
   d. Thank the receiver of your feedback for his or her contribution.

4. a. Describe the behavior or performance you want to redirect.
b. Listen to the other person's response.
c. Clarify your expectations or provide examples to illustrate your points.
d. Help your feedback recipient acknowledge that a problem exists and take responsibility for his or her actions.
e. Develop a plan for future action.
f. Thank your feedback recipient.
5. True

Chapter 5 Review (page 77)

1. True
2. True
3. True
4. False—Eye contact is important in any face-to-face encounter. Try to maintain eye contact with the person giving you feedback, even if you feel awkward.
5. a. Ask for details.
b. Paraphrase what you think you heard.
c. Seek suggestions for future action.
d. Thank the person for his or her feedback.
6. True
7. True

Chapter 6 Review (page 85)

1. d
2. a
3. c
4. b
5. Your own style
6. The other person's communication style